DK Eye Wonder

Explorer

LONDON, NEW YORK, MUNICH,
MELBOURNE, and DELHI

Written and edited by Marie Greenwood
Designed by Helen Chapman
Design assistant Gemma Fletcher

Publishing manager Susan Leonard
Jacket designer Emy Manby
Jacket editor Mariza O'Keeffe
Jacket copywriter Adam Powley
Picture researcher Liz Moore
Production Seyhan Esen-Yagmurlu
DTP designer Almudena Díaz
Consultant Peter Chrisp

Published in the United States by
DK Publishing, Inc.
375 Hudson Street
New York, New York 10014

06 07 08 09 10 10 9 8 7 6 5 4 3 2 1

ISBN-13 978-0-7566-1978-7
ISBN-10 0-7566-1978-5

Color reproduction by Colourscan, Singapore
Printed and bound in Italy by L.E.G.O.

Discover more at
www.dk.com

Contents

in deep space...

on snowy
mountaintops...

What is an explorer?

People have always wondered about faraway places. Explorers are people who decide to set out and discover them. Their reasons for traveling vary, but they always hope to return to tell exciting stories of the discoveries they have made...

at the bottom
of the sea...

across hot
desert lands...

Lure of gold

Explorers were often tempted by the gold, silver, and precious gemstones just waiting to be found in distant lands.

Nature

Some explorers journeyed to find new types of plants and animals. These discoveries increased people's knowledge of the world around them.

Challenge

Exploring can also be about testing yourself. Some people like the challenge of climbing the highest mountains.

Trade

One of the most important reasons for exploring was to find valued goods, such as spices, in distant countries.

Religion

Many early European explorers forced their own customs and beliefs on the peoples they conquered.

Mayan temple, Mexico

5

Who were they?

This map of the world was created thanks to the great journeys of many brave explorers. Whether traveling on foot, by camel, or by boat, they shared a strong sense of adventure.

Viking raiders from Scandinavia sought out new lands across the Atlantic Ocean. Erik the Red went to Iceland, and his son Leif Eriksson journeyed to North America.

Italian seaman Christopher Columbus set sail for Asia, but found North America instead.

American adventurers Meriwether Lewis and William Clark traveled by canoe along the rivers of North America in the early 19th century.

Spanish conquerer Francisco Pizarro set sail to South America and found the magnificent Inca Empire of Peru.

Portuguese nobleman Ferdinand Magellan led the first expedition that sailed all around the world.

Far and wide

This map shows some of the great explorers throughout history, and where they went to. Find out more about these and other brave travelers on the following pages.

Portuguese sea captain Vasco da Gama became the first European to reach India by sea in 1498.

The great Muslim traveler Ibn Battuta traveled throughout northern Africa and parts of Asia.

British seaman Captain Cook sailed to eastern Australia and New Zealand.

Scottish missionary Dr. David Livingstone explored the great African rivers.

In 1911, Norwegian explorer Roald Amundsen became the first person to reach the South Pole.

Early explorers

People have always gone on long journeys. The first travelers left Africa to look for new places to live. Later, explorers went on journeys to trade with other people.

Sea traders

The best seafarers of the ancient world, the Phoenicians built their ships using cedar trees from their native land of Lebanon in the Middle East.

Queen Hatshepsut of Egypt

Queen Hatshepsut's fleet of ships journeyed to the land of Punt, in Africa. They brought back many riches, such as ivory and ebony.

Egyptian relief from Queen Hatshepsut's chapel

JASON THE EXPLORER

Many ancient Greek legends were inspired by real journeys of exploration. The legend of Jason's search for a golden fleece, or sheepskin, may be based on truth. Ancient people living to the northeast of Greece used sheepskins to trap the gold from water flowing in their streams.

Chinese explorers

Chinese traveler Chang Chi'en trekked along the dusty Silk Road to central Asia and brought back news of distant lands.

Chang Chi'en led a hundred men from China to central Asia.

Viking voyages

The Vikings from northern Europe were fearsome fighters who often raided neighboring countries. When they wanted more room to settle, they turned to exploring.

Erik the Red

Viking explorer Erik the Red had a fiery temper. After killing several men, he had to flee his home in Iceland.

GREENLAND

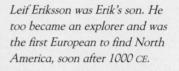

Erik encouraged many Icelanders to settle in Greenland.

Leif Eriksson was Erik's son. He too became an explorer and was the first European to find North America, soon after 1000 CE.

NORTH
AMERICA

Green land?

Erik the Red finally settled in a land covered in ice. It was even harsher than Iceland, but Erik named it Greenland to try and persuade people to settle there.

Viking riches

The Vikings were warriors before they were explorers. They raided lands and became rich in gold and silver.

ICELAND

Erik the Red and his family left Iceland to explore farther west.

SCANDINAVIA

Knarr ships

When exploring, the Vikings sailed in wide-bottomed ships called *knarrs*. Though slower than slim Viking warships, they had more room.

The wide square sail could be used to cover the knarr when moored, rather like a tent.

The Vikings set sail from Scandinavia, and, guided by flights of birds, eventually came to Iceland.

Arabian adventures

In the 14th century, the Muslim world spread far and wide. Muslims, followers of the faith of Islam, were highly educated. They also loved to travel, and none more so than brave adventurer Ibn Battuta.

Mecca

Ibn Battuta's main reason for traveling was to visit the holy site of Mecca, the birthplace of Islam, as all Muslims seek to do.

Ibn Battuta

Ibn Battuta journeyed for nearly 30 years across Asia and north Africa. He covered about 75,000 miles (120,000 km)—about the same as three times around the world.

"The Egyptian Nile surpasses all of the Earth." Ibn Battuta

Setting sail

Arab explorers and traders sailed across the seas in small boats called *dhows*. They are still used in the Middle East today.

The dhow's triangular sails help it sail close to the wind.

Astrolabe

The Arab people were great navigators. They developed the astrolabe, which helped sailors plot their position at sea by measuring the height of the Sun.

River view

Ibn Battuta sailed on a *dhow* along the Nile River in Egypt and was captivated by everything he saw.

SINBAD THE SAILOR

The daring exploits of Arab seafarers may have inspired the tales of Sinbad the sailor—a major character in the group of stories known as *The Arabian Nights*. One story tells how Sinbad was taken captive by the Old Man of the Sea and had to use great cunning to set himself free.

Journey into China

In the 13th century, Italian explorer Marco Polo arrived in Asia and journeyed along the dry, dusty track known as the Silk Road into China. When he eventually arrived at the court of the emperor Kublai Khan, he had been traveling for more than three years.

Marco Polo was only 16 when he set sail from Venice with his father and uncle.

The Polo family began their travels through Asia at Acre in the Middle East.

Camel travel

Like other merchants, Marco Polo traveled by camel train along the Silk Road. The route was a dangerous one—bandits lurked around every corner.

MARCO MILLIONS

On his return to Italy, Marco Polo told the stories of his travels. Some of his tales are extraordinary. He told of enormous birds that dropped elephants from a great height, and then ate them. He told of a city that had thousands of bridges. These far-fetched tales earned him the title "Marco Millions."

"I only told half of what I saw."
Marco Polo

Paper money
Marco Polo was amazed to see Chinese people using paper money in place of gold and silver.

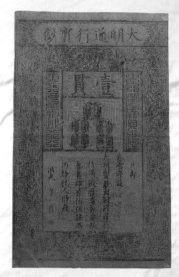

CHINA

Marco Polo arrived at the court of the Chinese emperor Kublai Khan.

Silk and spices
Silk and all kinds of spices were traded along the Silk Road. Silk was especially valuable—for centuries only the Chinese knew how to make it.

INDIA

Great Wall of China
Marco Polo does not mention the Great Wall or tea drinking in his travel stories, and some people think that he never even went to China. We will never know for sure.

The high seas

In the 1400s, European sailors set out on long ocean voyages. Their goal was to reach Asia. The continent was rich in spices, gold, jewels, and silk—treasures that the Europeans were desperate to get hold of.

Columbus

Vasco da Gama

East or west?
Two explorers set out in opposite directions to find Asia. First, Italian seaman Christopher Columbus sailed west, then Portuguese captain Vasco da Gama sailed south and east.

I saw three ships
Columbus took three ships on his voyage to America. The largest was the *Santa Maria*.

Wrong continent
Columbus did not make it to Asia, but he did find America. He never realized his mistake and thought he had reached the Indies (the old name for Asia). That is thought to be why Native Americans are sometimes called "Indians."

SOUTH AMERICA

ASIA

"At a very tender age, I went to sea sailing, and so I have continued to this day."

Christopher Columbus

INDIA

AFRICA

New wildlife
On reaching Cuba, Columbus saw turtles and flamingos for the first time.

Into India
Vasco da Gama was the first European to travel to India by sea. He saw many strange animals, including rhinoceroses and elephants.

Around the world

Without really meaning to, Portuguese explorer Ferdinand Magellan led the first voyage around the world. As a result, the true size of the Earth was revealed, and it was proved once and for all that we live on a round planet.

Setting sail
Magellan's goal was to find a route to the Spice Islands of Asia. He offered his services to the king of Spain, and his expedition set off in 1518.

Journey end
After three years at sea, Magellan's ship, the *Victoria*, returned home safely. It was now captained by Spanish seaman Juan del Cano.

SOUTH AMERICA

Magellan referred to the calm waters of the Pacific as the "sea of peace."

This early map shows the Strait of Magellan through which Magellan sailed.

Narrow passage
Magellan is said to have wept for joy when he came through the dangerous, stormy passage at the tip of South America that is now named after him.

Tragic end

Sadly, Magellan never completed the journey. He was killed in a battle in the Philippines.

Caravel

Portuguese explorers sailed in small wooden sailing ships called caravels. Their smaller size made it easier to explore the coastlines of the world.

Only one of Magellan's fleet of five ships survived the journey.

"After a voyage of more than three years, we have arrived."

Juan del Cano

Round world

After Magellan's voyage, people knew the size and shape of the Earth, and accurate globes could be made.

A sailor's work

Sailors climbed high masts to check ropes and repair sails. They washed down decks and took turns keeping watch.

Even when storms raged, sailors still had to work the sails.

A seafarer's life

Life on board ship was tough for sailors of long ago. Voyages could stretch on for months, even into years. Sailors had no fresh food to eat. The work was long and hard.

Cat-o'nine-tails

If a sailor disobeyed orders, he would be punished. One method was to be whipped with a "cat-o'nine-tails."

The cat-o'nine-tails is a whip with nine pieces of rope.

A sailor's feast

It was impossible to store fresh food for long. Sailors feasted on ship's biscuits that would keep for years, but which were often infested with maggots.

Hammocks swing sideways so they do not tip out sleeping sailors.

Slumber party

If they were lucky, sailors slept in hammocks, which protected them from the rat-infested, wet decks below.

Disease

With dirty conditions and no fresh food to eat, sailors could catch a disease called scurvy. This led to many sailors dying at sea.

Keeping track

When sailors were at sea with no land in sight, they had a problem: how did they know where they were? By using different navigation methods, they were able to figure out which way to go.

Star guide
In the early days, sailors looked to the sky and, with the help of a crosstaff, used the position of the stars and the Sun to guide them.

Log books were often beautifully drawn.

The needle on a compass, pulled by the Earth's magnetism, always points north.

The coast of Africa was mapped in detail before its interior, where travel was more difficult.

Compass

By the 1400s, sailors had begun to use tools such as the compass to help them plot their journey.

Mapping it out

Many explorers made maps of the areas they traveled to. This early map of Africa shows the coastline in detail.

Captain's log

Each day the ship's captain wrote down in a log book how far and in which direction the ship had traveled.

Eye spy

By peering through a telescope, an explorer could spot landmarks from a great distance.

Early English telescope

Gold Aztec mask

from Mexico

Greed for gold
The Spanish conquerors, or
conquistadors, melted down
hundreds of beautiful gold
objects in order to take
them back to Spain.

Quest for gold

When Spanish explorers reached Central and South America they came across cultures very different from their own. The Spanish did not understand these peoples, but they did want their gold.

Cortes the god

When the Aztec people of Mexico first saw explorer Hernan Cortes, they thought he was a god. But Cortes had come to conquer them.

Temple worship

Cortes was appalled by the Aztec practice of sacrificing humans to their gods. He ordered that temples be destroyed. Later, the Aztecs were converted to Christianity.

Peaceful people

Explorer Francisco Pizarro was peacefully received by the Inca people of Peru. But, like the Aztecs, they were soon under attack. Armed with guns, the Spanish found it easy to overcome both peoples, whose weapons were more basic.

The Incas lived high in the Andes Mountains.

Aztec spear

Into America

In 1804 two Americans, Lewis and Clark, set out from St. Louis to explore western North America. They braved grizzly bears, wild rivers, and rugged mountain ranges on their quest to open up this land, known only to the Native Americans who lived there.

Lewis and Clark
US President Thomas Jefferson sent Lewis and Clark to explore the American west. This was land that had recently been bought by the US.

Their journey
Lewis and Clark traveled from St. Louis by canoe, following the river routes until they came to the Pacific Ocean.

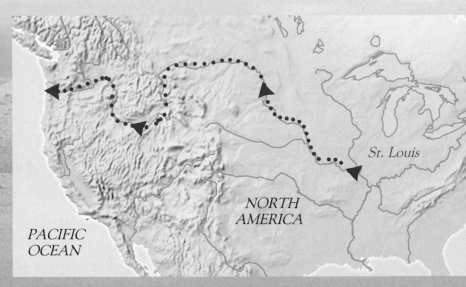

PACIFIC OCEAN

St. Louis

NORTH AMERICA

Wild animals
Lewis and Clark were amazed to see great herds of buffalo roaming the plains of North America.

Native Americans passed around pipes such as these as a sign of peace.

Peace pipe

Generally, Lewis and Clark got along well with the Native peoples they met. They often smoked a pipe of peace with them.

Bear chase

Lewis and Clark were very scared at one stage—they were chased into a river by an angry brown bear. It took several bullets to kill it.

Paddle power

The best way to travel into North America was by canoe along the many rivers that cross this vast land.

Explorers traveled in canoes made of birchbark, which were light and easy to handle.

BIRD WOMAN

Sacagawea, whose name means "Bird Woman," was a Native American woman from the Shoshone tribe. She joined Lewis and Clark on their journey and became their guide and interpreter.

Into the jungle

In the 1800s, Africa offered a real challenge to the bravest explorer. There was the threat of catching tropical diseases or being attacked by wild animals. But Scottish explorer David Livingstone was determined to go there.

Dr. Livingstone
David Livingstone was a doctor and a missionary. He wanted to go to Africa to help people.

Mighty waterfall
Livingstone found a huge waterfall called *Mosi Oa Tunya* ("smoke that thunders"). He renamed it Victoria Falls after Britain's Queen Victoria.

The Nile
Livingstone went in seach of the source of the Nile River, but never found it. And when explorer John Speke found its source at Lake Victoria, no one believed him at first.

River travel
The best way to explore Africa was by boat, though this could be dangerous. Once, Livingstone's boat was capsized by a hippopotamus.

"Dr. Livingstone, I presume?"

Henry Stanley on meeting Dr. Livingstone

Meeting up

At one stage, Livingstone was thought to have gone missing. It was American Henry Mortan Stanley who finally found him.

The South Seas

For years, the eastern coast of Australia was a mystery, and people thought the two islands of New Zealand were one. Then in the late 1700s, Captain James Cook set sail from England...

Mapping it out

Captain Cook was a fine map drawer, or cartographer. He drew detailed maps of the Pacific Ocean.

Captain Cook

Captain Cook set sail from Plymouth. His mission was to chart the unknown regions of the South Pacific.

The Maori tattooed their faces with elaborate patterns.

Paradise island

On his first voyage, Cook sailed to Tahiti, and the lush beauty of the island seemed like paradise.

Honest people

Cook won the trust of the Maori people of New Zealand. He described the Maori as strong, honest, and brave.

Life on board ship was good for Captain Cook's men. Nourishing food was served, and the ship was kept spotless.

KANGAROO HOP

On arriving in Australia, Cook was amazed to see kangaroos for the first time. He wrote in his journal, "I should have taken it for a wild dog... but it jumped like a hare."

Endeavour

Cook's ship the *Endeavour* was a cat-collier, one that was normally used to carry coal. Though not fast moving, the ship was very strong.

Exploring nature

In the 1800s, explorers sought new challenges. Experts in plants and animals, called naturalists, set out to find out more about the wonders of the natural world.

Mary Kingsley

Back then, it was unusual for women to travel alone, but British explorer Mary Kingsley longed to leave her safe home and go in search of adventure.

Into Africa

Mary Kingsley ventured deep into African swamp land to look for rare fish and insects. She faced many dangers. Her canoe was capsized several times and was once attacked by a crocodile.

"The swamp is full of noises... and creaking and groaning sounds from the trees."

Mary Kingsley

Charles Darwin

Naturalist Charles Darwin was only 22 years old when he set off to explore the South Atlantic and South Pacific. He was to make many important discoveries.

Exotic plants

Explorers discovered new plant species that grew in different environments, such as tropical rain forests in South America.

This species of palm tree grows in Brazil.

Beetles that Darwin collected on his journey

Specimens

Darwin collected many small animals and insects and studied them through his microscope.

Detailed drawings

Before photography, in order to record what they found, naturalists needed to be able to draw. These butterfly drawings are by explorer Henry Bates.

Henry Bates discovered hundreds of new butterfly species in South America.

To the North Pole

American explorer Robert Peary was determined to reach the North Pole. On one of many failed attempts, he got terrible frostbite, and his toes broke off.

Frostbitten fingers

"A few toes aren't much to give to achieve the Pole."

Robert Peary

Like the Inuits, Robert Peary wore sealskin as protection from the freezing cold.

Fellow traveler

Matthew Henson was an invaluable companion to Peary on his expeditions. He was a skilled navigator and sled-driver, and could speak the local Inuit language.

Poles apart

Roald Amundsen

Winners and losers

Scott and his team did make it to the South Pole, but a Norwegian flag was already there. Amundsen had won the race. Tired and dejected, Scott's team started on their return journey. But they never made it home.

Captain Robert Scott longed to be the first person to reach the South Pole.

Pole prize

Peary tried and tried again, and, in 1909, finally achieved his lifelong ambition to reach the North Pole.

Peary, Henson, and the rest of the team at the North Pole

By the late 19th century, explorers had traveled to most parts of the world—but the far reaches of the North and South poles still remained an icy mystery.

Race to the Pole

The Norwegian team was the best equipped. While they had skis and dog sleds, the British team hauled its sleds by hand.

To the South Pole

On the other side of the world from the Arctic north is the vast frozen continent of Antarctica. In 1911, two teams set out to reach the South Pole: a Norwegian team led by Roald Amundsen and a British team led by Robert Scott.

The Norwegians used husky dogs to pull their sleds.

Mapping the deep

For many years, the ocean depths remained a mystery. People are not made to travel under water, and they need special equipment to help them. But, as diving technology developed, so people were able to explore a wondrous, watery world.

Hold your breath

The earliest divers held their breath when swimming under water, so could only stay below the surface for a few minutes. But the invention of the first diver's helmet allowed divers to stay under water for longer.

Early diving helmets were made of copper and were very heavy. Air was pumped into the helmet through a pipe.

On the seabed

Shipwrecks and sunken treasure have been found at the bottom of the sea. In 1985, the wreck of the *Titanic* was discovered.

SEA CREATURES

The underwater world was once shrouded in mystery. Sailors would tell stories of all kinds of sea creatures, including mermaids combing their hair and singing songs that lured men to their deaths.

Deeper and deeper...

Divers were able to go deep under the sea in this strange steel ball, called a bathysphere. They saw all kinds of amazing fish never seen before.

Aqualungs are tanks of compressed air.

Swimming freely

The invention of the aqualung meant that divers could swim freely underwater for long periods, just as fish do.

Underwater life

Deep down on the ocean floor, hot springs called hydrothermal vents have been found, teeming with life including tube worms, clams, and blind crabs.

Tube worms

Reaching for the sky

Exploring is also about facing extreme challenges. By the 1900s, people turned their eyes upward to the highest mountains in the world, and sought to conquer them.

Peak success

People longed to climb Mount Everest, the world's highest mountain. In 1953, New Zealander Edmund Hillary and Tenzing Norgay from Tibet became the first people to reach the summit.

"A few more whacks of the ice-ax... and we stood on the top."

Edmund Hillary

Tragic climb

For years, the Matterhorn peak in the European Alps seemed impossible to climb. Edward Whymper finally succeeded on the eighth attempt, but, tragically, four of his companions fell to their deaths on the way down.

Lost explorer

George Mallory was determined to climb Everest. On the third attempt he disappeared. Years later, Mallory's body and some of his belongings were found.

Mallory's goggles

No one knows if Mallory ever reached the summit.

Gripping stuff

The jagged edge of an ice-ax is essential for a climber since it grips ice and snow.

YETI—FRIEND OR FOE?

In the snowy mountains of the Himalayas, explorers have reported finding huge footprints in the snow, believed to belong to the abominable snowman, or yeti. Some say that this strange creature attacked them, others claim he helped them. But no one knows if the yeti even exists.

Space race

For centuries, people dreamed about traveling into space and exploring distant planets. But it was not until the late 1950s that the United States and the Soviet Union battled to be the first nation to send a person deep into space.

Sputnik 1

The space race really began with the launch by the Soviets of the first artificial satellite *Sputnik 1* in 1957. It orbited Earth every 96 minutes.

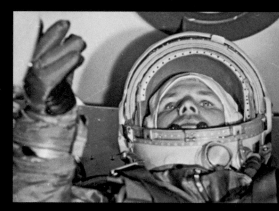

First in space

When *Vostok 1* powered into orbit in 1961, Soviet astronaut Yuri Gagarin was strapped inside. He was the first human to enter space.

Footprint

Footprints made by Armstrong and Aldrin will remain on the Moon for millions of years, since there is no wind to remove them.

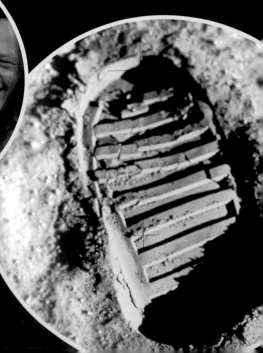

First on the Moon

In 1969, three American astronauts—Neil Armstrong, Edwin Aldrin, and Michael Collins—blasted off from Earth in *Apollo 11*. Their mission was to reach the Moon.

The command module inside Apollo 11 was called Columbia, named after Italian explorer Christopher Columbus.

> *"That's one small step for man —one giant leap for mankind."*
>
> Neil Armstrong

Moon walk

Neil Armstrong opened the hatch.
He climbed down the ladder
one step at a time.
He stepped onto the
surface of the Moon.
He was the first man
on the Moon.

*Six hundred million
people watched the
first Moon walk on
TV, from the safety
of their own homes.*

On to Mars!

People have been fascinated by Mars for centuries, and have longed to set foot on this red planet—the closest one to Earth. In 1976, the first mission to Mars took place—but only robots, not people, landed there. These robots were the Viking landers. Further expeditions followed, but no life-form has been found on Mars.

Viking invasion

The Viking landers took a year to reach Mars. They studied the climate on Mars, took pictures, and sent them back to Earth.

The lander's robotic arm scoops up soil and looks for signs of life.

The Rovers trek about 130 ft (40 m) across the surface in a day, analyzing rocks and soils.

The Viking landers took the first ever pictures of the surface of Mars.

LIFE ON MARS

Mars has often been seen as a possible threat to Earth. The novelist H. G. Wells came up with the idea of a Martian invasion of Earth in his book, *The War of the Worlds.*

The dry, dusty landscape makes it look like a hot desert, but Mars is in fact freezing cold.

Mars surface

Mars is known as the red planet because of the rusty-red dust that lies on its surface.

The Rovers are still on Mars today.

Rover

Twin Mars Exploration Rovers reached Mars in 2004. They landed on opposite sides of the planet.

Hubble telescope

Exploring space is not just about visiting planets, it is also about observing. The Hubble Space Telescope helps people find out new things about the universe.

Hidden nature

Naturalists continue to find
and study new species of plants
and animals hidden in the
"canopy" of leaves that towers
above the rain forest floor.

Today's explorers

Today, most of the world is known and charted, and exploring has become more about endurance and breaking records than discovering new places.

Exploring the past

Exploring can also be about making great discoveries from the past. British archeologist Howard Carter found the tomb of Egyptian pharaoh Tutankhamun in 1922.

An amazing collection of gold and ebony treasures were unearthed in Tutankhamun's tomb.

Desert roamer

Australian Robyn Davidson trekked across the Australian desert for six months with four camels and a dog for company.

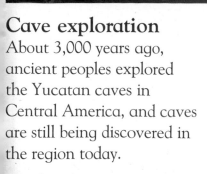

Cave exploration

About 3,000 years ago, ancient peoples explored the Yucatan caves in Central America, and caves are still being discovered in the region today.

Across ice and sand

Explorer Ranulph Fiennes journeyed around the world crossing both North and South poles. He also found the legendary Lost City of Ubar in the Arabian desert.

Explorers

This timeline lists the explorers found in this book, when and where they explored, and the page numbers on which they can be found.

Queen Hatshepsut *Egyptian 9*
c. 1490 BCE Sailed from Egypt to Punt in Africa

Chang Chi'en *Chinese 9*
138-160 BCE Trekked along the Silk Road in central Asia

Erik the Red *Norse 6, 10*
980s CE Sailed from Iceland to Greenland

Leif Eriksson *Norse 6, 10*
1000s CE Sailed from Greenland to North America

Marco Polo *Italian 14-15*
1271-91 Traveled across Asia to China

Ibn Battuta *Moroccan 7, 12-13*
1324-53 Traveled across Asia and north Africa

Christopher Columbus *Italian 6, 16-17*
1492-1504 Sailed from Europe to the Americas

Vasco da Gama *Portuguese 7, 16-17*
1497-98 Sailed from Portugal to India

Ferdinand Magellan *Portuguese 6, 18-19*
1519-22 Led the first voyage around the world

Hernan Cortes *Spanish 25*
1519-21 Conquered the Aztec people of Mexico

Francisco Pizarro *Spanish 6, 25*
1531-33 Conquered the Inca people of Peru

James Cook *English 7, 30-31*
1768-79 Sailed to the South Pacific

William Clark *American 6, 26-27*
1804-06 Traveled by canoe across North America

Meriwether Lewis *American 6, 26-27*
1804-06 Traveled by canoe across North America

Charles Darwin *English 33*
1831-36 Naturalist who explored around South America

David Livingstone *Scottish 7, 28-29*
1841-73 Journeyed into Africa

Henry Bates *English 33*
1848-59 Naturalist who explored South America

John Speke *English 28*
1854-1860 Discovered the source of the Nile River

Edward Whymper *English 39*
1865 Climbed the Matterhorn in Europe

Henry Morton Stanley *American 29*
1871-89 Journeyed into Africa

Matthew Henson *American 34-35*
1908-09 Explored the Arctic; first to reach the North Pole

Robert Peary *American 34-35*
1908-09 Explored the Arctic; first to reach the North Pole

Mary Kingsley *English 32*
1893-1900 Naturalist who explored West Africa

Roald Amundsen *Norwegian 7, 34-35*
1910-12 Explored the Antarctic; first to reach the South Pole

Robert Scott *English 34-35*
1910-12 Explored the Antarctic

George Mallory *English 39*
1920s Mountaineer who died on Mt. Everest

Howard Carter *English 45*
1922 Archeologist who discovered Tutankhamun's tomb

Edmund Hillary *New Zealander 38*
1953 First to climb Mt. Everest

Tenzing Norgay *Tibetan 38*
1953 First to climb Mt. Everest

Yuri Gagarin *Russian 40*
1961 First man in space

Neil Armstrong *American 40-41*
1969 First man on the Moon

Robyn Davidson *Australian 45*
1977 Trekked across the Australian desert

Ranulph Fiennes *English 45*
1992 Explored across North and South poles

Glossary

Here are the meanings of some words it is useful to know when learning about explorers.

Astrolabe an early navigation tool that shows the position of the planets and stars.

Caravel a small Spanish or Portuguese ship of the 15th and 16th centuries.

Cartographer a person who draws maps.

Cat-collier a ship used to carry coal.

Conquistador Spanish conqueror of the Americas.

Crosstaff an early navigation tool that measured the position of the stars.

Dhow an Arab boat with triangular sails.

Inuit native peoples of northern Canada, Alaska, and Greenland.

Interpreter a person who translates for people so that they can speak to each other in different languages.

Knarr a wide-bottomed Viking ship.

Log book a book that holds a record of a ship's progress.

Navigation to figure out the position, course, and distance traveled.

Naturalist a person who studies plants and animals.

North Pole the northernmost point on Earth.

Scurvy a disease caused by a lack of vitamin C.

Settler a person who goes to live in a previously uninhabited or sparsely populated area.

Source the point of origin of a stream or river.

South Pole the southernmost point on Earth.

Swamp an area of wet, marshy land.

Uncharted an area of land not recorded on a map or chart.

Yeti Legendary monster believed to live in the Himalyas.

Index

Acknowledgments

Dorling Kindersley would like to thank:
Anthony Limerick for design inspiration; Carrie Love and Fleur Star for editorial assistance; and Liz Moore for picture research.

Picture credits

The publisher would like to thank the following for their kind permission to reproduce their photographs:
a=above; c=center; b=below; l=left; r=right; t=top
akg-images: 19br; **Alamy Images:** Aqua Image 44b; Danita Delimont 16br; Stephen Frink 4bl; Robert Harding Picture Library Ltd. 10c, 10cr, 11cra, 11b, 30l; Stock Montage Inc. 6crb; Poppefoto 34bl, 34bc; Helene Rogers 14b; Royal Geographical Society 45br; World Religions Photo Library 12cl; **The Art Archive:** Marine Museum Lisbon/Dagli Orti 6cra, 6bl, 16tc, 18tl, 25tl; Dagli Orti 8tr; Museo de Arte Antiga Lisbon/Dagli Orti 7tl, 16tr; Bibliotheque Nationale, Paris 8-9b; Culver Pictures 34tl; Private Collection/Marc Charmet 7clb; www.bridgeman.co.uk: 33tl; British Museum 27tl; Peter Newark American Pictures 6cl, 26tl; **Corbis:** 7b, 16bl, 18bl, 19bl, 41; Peter Adams 19tr; James L. Amos 26-27cb; Yann Arthus-Bertrand 4br; Dave Bartruff 5cl; Philip de Bay 18b; Tom Bean 26-27b; Bettmann 15tr, 22l, 34tc, 35ca, 40tl, 40clb; Stefano Bianchetti 28cl; Tibor Bognar 4tr; Werner Forman 9t; Lowell Georgia 43tl; Historical Picture Archive 19tl; Thom Lang 48 (suitcase); Frans Lanting 30b; Wally Mcnamee 40bl; NASA/Roger Ressmeyer 42l; Royalty-Free 16bl;

Reuters 16cl; Joel W. Rogers 20l; Galen Rowell 34-35b; Stapleton Collection 1; David Stoecklein 15tl; Sygma 39tr; Karl Weatherly 39tl; Ralph White 37tl; Zefa 4tl; **DK Image Library:** Peter Anderson © Danish National Museum 10tr, 11tr; British Museum 25r; courtesy of Darwin Collection, The Home of Charles Darwin, Down House (English Heritage) 33c; James Stevenson © Dorling Kindersley, courtesy of the National Maritime Museum, London 13tl; Alan Hills © The British Museum 16tc; **Empics Ltd.:** AP 31, 36-37c, 45tr; **Werner Forman Archive:** 27c; **Getty Images:** Theo Allofs 44t; Altrendo 32; Per Breiehagen 34-35t; Robert Caputo 13tr; DE Cox 15br; Macduff Everton 45cb; J. P. Fruchet 2-3; Raymond Gehman 28br; Sylvain Grandadam 28bl; Jon Gray 12-13b; Nick Greaves 28-29cr; Hulton Archive 29r, 45ca; Photos Images 5b; Jonathan Kantor 39br; Alan Kearney 5r; National Geographic 8tl, 46-47; Harald Sund 10br; Taxi 29bl; Time Life Pictures 35bl; Konrad Wothe 27tr; **NASA:** 40br, 43tr; © **National Maritime Museum, London:** 21tr, 21cl, 22b, 23cla, 23c, 30c; Greenwich Hospital Collection 7cr, 30tc; **National Geographic Image Collection:** Gordon Wiltsie 35br; **The Natural History Museum, London:** 33b; naturepl.com: Ashish & Shanthi Chandola 17br; **Photolibrary. com:** Oxford Scientific Films 33r; **Royal Geographical Society Picture Library:** George Lowe 38-39; **Science & Society Picture Library:** Science Museum 23b; **Science Photo Library:** Custom Medical Stock Photo 34tr; NASA 42-43b, 43br; Novosti 40ca; **South American Pictures:** Tony Morrision 25c, 25bl; Chris Sharp 24; **Still Pictures:** Roland Seitre 32cl; **Superstock:** Lehn 22-23t, 48 (stars); **TopFoto.co.uk:** 32tl, 33tc; The Image Works 20tr; Roger Viollet 14tl; **Woods Hole Oceanographic Institition:** 37br

All other images © Dorling Kindersley

For further information see: www.dkimages.com